# RAILS
# AROUND
# DUBLIN

An Irish Railway Pictorial

Dónal Murray

Midland Publishing

**Rails Around Dublin: An Irish Railway Pictorial**
Dónal Murray © 2002

ISBN 1 85780 144 X

First published in 2002 by Midland Publishing
4 Watling Drive, Hinckley, Leics, LE10 3EY, England.
Tel: 01455 233 747  Fax: 01455 233 737
E-mail: midlandbooks@compuserve.com

Design concept and layout
© Midland Publishing and
Stephen Thompson Associates

Midland Publishing is an imprint of
Ian Allan Publishing Ltd.

Printed in England by Ian Allan Printing Ltd
Riverdene Business Park, Hersham, Surrey, KT12 4RG

Front cover: **A CIE AEC railcar set heading south across the loop line viaduct in the late 1960s.** Ian Allan Library

Title Page: **Former GSR 2-6-2T No 850 pauses between suburban duties at Dun Laoghaire in the 1950s.** Seán Kennedy

## CONTENTS

# INTRODUCTION

The city of Dublin and its hinterland has witnessed many radical changes in the historically short period of time since Dublin's and indeed Ireland's first passenger train steamed out of Westland Row on 17th December 1834 on the Dublin & Kingstown Railway. Following that historic occasion, something of a railway building mania soon gripped Dublin and the entire country. At its peak, the Irish railway system eventually amounted to some 3,442 route miles and employed more than 19,000 people by the 1920s. To fully understand how Dublin's railways have evolved since the 1830s, it is necessary to take a brief look at some of the physical, political and railway developments that have occurred since that time.

By the early 1920s Dublin had five main railway stations owned by four separate companies which themselves had grown out of the amalgamations or absorptions of many different companies. The aforementioned Dublin & Kingstown Railway had been leased by an agreement of 1846 to the Waterford, Wexford, Wicklow & Dublin Railway which in turn became the Dublin & Wicklow Railway, the Dublin, Wicklow & Wexford Railway and finally, in 1907, the Dublin & South Eastern Railway. The DSER therefore operated out of the original Dublin & Kingstown terminus at Westland Row which had become a through station with the opening of the City of Dublin Junction Railway's loop line in 1891. This line connected Westland Row to the Great Northern Railway at Amiens Street. The DSER's other main station in the city was the former Dublin & Wicklow Railway's terminus at Harcourt Street.

Over on the west side of the city, Ireland's biggest railway company, the Great Southern & Western, was based at the architecturally significant Kingsbridge station. The GSWR thought of itself as Ireland's premier line. Its main line out of Dublin had opened to Carlow in 1846 and reached a temporary terminus at Blackpool, on the northern outskirts of Cork, in 1849. GSWR trains later served such places as Waterford, Limerick, Tralee, Athlone and Sligo. By the end of the nineteenth century, it had become, by some way, the largest railway company on the island. Much of this growth was achieved by absorbing smaller railway concerns and some large ones such as the Waterford, Limerick & Western Railway, whose tracks ran from that south eastern port, to Sligo in the north west.

Broadstone, the Dublin terminus of the Midland Great Western Railway, occupied an elevated site north-west of the city centre. Like its rival the GSWR, the Midland, as it was commonly known, absorbed or operated many smaller railway concerns. Its main line reached Galway in 1851 and later places served included Westport, Sligo and Cavan along with remote locations on the west coast such as Clifden, Achill and Killala.

The final railway serving the city of Dublin was the Great Northern operating out of its imposing Amiens Street station which had been built originally as the southern terminus of the Dublin & Drogheda Railway. The D&D was also partly responsible for the unusual gauge which is used in Ireland. Ireland's first railway, the Dublin & Kingstown, was built to what later became the international standard gauge of 4ft 8½in (1435mm). In the 1840s, railways across the Irish Sea in Britain, were being built to both that standard gauge and Brunel's broad gauge of 7ft 0¼in. The British government, alarmed at the disruption which this was causing, decided to try and nip this problem in the bud as far as Ireland was concerned at least. A government appointed commission was set up to establish the best gauge for Ireland's railways. The commission decided on a gauge of 6ft 2in and this was adopted by the Ulster Railway which was building a line from Belfast to Armagh. This would ultimately join with lines going north from Dublin to form a connection between the two cities.

The Dublin & Drogheda however, decided to ignore the new gauge and proposed using a gauge of 5ft 2in for its line north from Dublin. There was now the prospect of a break of gauge on the main Dublin to Belfast railway. Eventually the Board of Trade took the matter in hand and ruled that the standard gauge for Ireland should be set at 5ft 3in (1600mm). A railway connecting the D&D and the UR, the Dublin & Belfast Junction Railway, completed the north-south link upon the opening of the first Boyne viaduct in 1855. This was quite not the end for the international standard gauge in Ireland as we shall see later, but for the moment we will return to the development of Dublin's railways.

The Great Northern Railway came into being in 1876 following the amalgamation of the Ulster Railway, the Dublin & Belfast Junction and the Dublin & Drogheda amongst others. From Amiens Street trains served a large part of the north west and north east of the island, including such diverse destinations as Derry, Bundoran, Enniskillen, Belfast, Navan and Howth. With the advent of the City of Dublin Junction Railways in 1891, a physical connection was made with the former Dublin, Wicklow & Wexford Railway's coastal route to the south-east. A further connection was also made with the MGWR line to the North Wall, at Newcomen Junction. The City of Dublin Junction Railways remained an independent company right up until the formation of the Great Southern Railways in 1925, although it never possessed any rolling stock and was worked by the DWWR and its successor, the DSER, throughout it's entire existence.

Each of the four large companies also had its own self contained locomotive, carriage and wagon works and all were located in Dublin except for the Great Northern Railway works which was at Dundalk. The DSER works was at Grand Canal Street, just outside Westland Row. This works had the distinction of being the first railway company owned establishment to turn out its own locomotive. The GSWR works were at Inchicore, approximately two miles west of Kingsbridge station. Inchicore was and is a quite massive complex, which over the years has turned out far more than just railway products. The MGWR's facility in Dublin was at Broadstone, located adjacent to the passenger and goods terminus of the same name.

Major goods depots or yards belonging to the four companies in Dublin were generally located at or adjacent to the main stations such as Harcourt Street, Kingsbridge, Broadstone and Amiens Street. However, there were other very important freight locations around the city including the MGWR's yard at Liffey Junction which primarily served the nearby cattle markets. The greatest concentration of yards was at the North Wall which had goods yards belonging to the Midland, the GSWR and the GNR. There was also a station and yard owned by the English London & North Western Railway close to its steamer berth though services to this station were worked by the Irish companies. The activities at North Wall are dealt with later in the book.

In and around Dublin, the DSER and the GNR, and to a more limited extent the GSWR, operated what would be termed today, suburban services. These were generally less intensive and important than those around British cities. The population of Ireland had been decimated by famine and economic decline in the nineteenth century. It virtually halved between 1841 and 1921, with emigration the only hope for thousands.

The partition of the island of Ireland after 1921 with the creation of the Irish Free State or Saorstát Éireann was also a contributory factor to the general economic situation, which affected the course of Irish and therefore Dublin's railway history. After partition many of the established trading routes were affected by the new international boundary. Customs posts were set up on the border and duties were imposed on various commodities by both sides further disrupting trade.

Civil war in the Free State also followed partition and lasted until 1923 with substantially more damage done to the railways in this period than in the war of independence from 1918 to 1921. The result of all of this war damage to the railways and the massive inflation in costs, particularly labour costs, which had occurred during the Great War and in the years leading up to the establishment of the Irish Free State, was that almost all of the railway companies in Ireland were in financial difficulties.

Solutions to Ireland's transport problems never came easy, but the Free State government recognised that something radical had to be done if the country itself was to become economically viable and this meant amongst other things, saving the railways. The Railways Act of July 1924 resulted in the amalgamation of the Great Southern & Western, the Midland Great Western and the Cork Bandon & South Coast Railway into a new company called the Great Southern Railway. After some lengthy negotiations the Dublin & South Eastern was also brought into the amalgamation on the 1st of January 1925. Several other smaller companies were also absorbed. The Great Southern Railway was then renamed, the Great Southern Railways.

Unfortunately the newly created GSR only took responsibility for railways lying wholly within the Irish Free State. Lines which crossed the border such as the Great Northern Railway, the Sligo Leitrim & Northern Counties Railway, the Dundalk, Newry & Greenore and Donegal's two narrow gauge systems, remained nominally independent until either dismemberment or complete closure. The GSR ran its share of Dublin's railways for the next 20 years. During its short life it made brave attempts to cut costs for example by singling most of the former Midland line to Galway in the 1920s, closing Broadstone as a passenger station and a locomotive works in 1937, though Broadstone remained open as a locomotive depot until 1961. The same fate had earlier befallen the DSER's Grand Canal Street works in 1925. A handful of very uneconomic lines were closed in the 1930s, such as the former Midland branches to Clifden and Achill. The GSR also, despite its limited funds, boldly experimented with new technology in the form of the Drumm Battery trains and electrically operated colour light signalling in parts of the Dublin area, and even managed to construct a handful of new suburban and main line locomotives and coaches.

By the end of the 'Emergency', as the Second World War period was known in the neutral Irish Free State, the GSR was on its last legs financially. Again the government was forced to act in the interests of maintaining transport within the state. The Transport Act of 1944 provided for the amalgamation of the GSR and the Dublin United Transport Company into a new enterprise. This of course brings the Dublin tramways into our story, which at one time was the largest tramway system in these islands.

The new company which came into being on 1st January 1945 was known as Córas Iompair Éireann or CIE. Although nominally a private company, CIE was provided with a mechanism which allowed for some exchequer funding. For the first time, the vast majority of rail and road services within the state were in the hands of one operator. In Dublin the only other large operator of road and rail services was the GNR. The future looked bright from a public transport perspective in 1945 as wartime restrictions and rationing, particularly of fuel, began to be lifted. Dieselisation of CIE rail services was soon mooted and five diesel shunting locomotives were ordered in 1945 and were later delivered from Inchicore works in 1947 and 1948. Equipment was also ordered for six twin-engined main line express locomotives and two mixed traffic locomotives. The later were delivered in 1950 and 1951. However, unforeseen events occurred yet again which affected the entire transport scene, both in Dublin and nationwide.

The winters of 1946 and 1947 were the worst in living memory across these islands. Rail services, along with many other aspects of life, were badly disrupted. Coal supplies which were almost entirely imported, virtually dried up and rail services were cut to the bone. Several steam locomotives were converted to oil burning as an emergency measure to keep a basic rail service operating. Unfortunately for CIE, the small profit that the company had shown at the end of 1945, was suddenly turned into a very large deficit by the end of 1947, a trend which was repeated in most of the following years. In 1948 another event of a different sort occurred which temporarily at least affected CIE's course and that of the transport scene in Dublin. A report commissioned by the Minister for Industry and Commerce into transport in Ireland, the Milne report, bizarrely recommended against the wholesale dieselisation of rail services, which it referred to as, 'unproven technology'. This recommendation seemed to ignore the disastrous affects of the recent coal shortages and the high maintenance and operating costs of steam locomotives. This report effectively put an end to the order for the twin-engined express locomotives as previously mentioned. By postponing dieselisation, it forced CIE to continue to try to maintain its services using an ageing fleet of steam locomotives. After the initial optimism, CIE was soon in the same financial bind which had characterised the GSR. Something had to be done urgently to try and improve the company's position.

Again the government entered the equation and with the passing of the Transport Act of 1950, CIE was nationalised becoming a phenomenon known as a semi-state company. At this time the Grand Canal Company was also merged with CIE, effectively bringing almost all land-based transportation operating wholly within the newly created Republic of Ireland, into the hands of the company. There was however, a serious flaw in the legislation, based on an improbable assumption. One of the provisions of the Transport Act of 1950 was that CIE would operate at a profit. Most of the company's losses stemmed from its rail services. To try and cut these losses a twofold strategy was pursued, many uneconomic or marginally economic rail lines were closed and on the positive side, a modernisation programme to dieselise rail services and provide much needed new rolling stock, was introduced. In relation to Dublin on the road services side, the last former DUTC, now CIE, tram operated on the No 8 route to Dalkey in 1949. Dublin city services were now completely in the hands of a growing fleet of relatively new buses.

However, the railway closures and cuts in service also spread to the capital. 1958 saw the closure of the line from Harcourt Street to Shanganagh Junction and a number of suburban stations on the former Dublin & Kingstown section also lost their services in these years. The closure of the Clonsilla to Navan line was completed in 1963.

This period also saw the final demise of the once powerful Great Northern Railway. By the early 1950s the GNR had itself reached a dire financial position and its directors threatened to suspend its services. In one of the few examples of cross border co-operation of the period, the governments in Belfast and Dublin both agreed to financially support the Great Northern Railway. In 1952 they created a Great Northern Railway Board, which had equal representation from the two governments, to run the system. This arrangement lasted until 1958 when the GNRB was disbanded. The assets of the company were equally distributed between CIE in the Republic and the Ulster Transport Authority in Northern Ireland. Thus CIE acquired approximately fifty percent of the GNR's locomotives, railcars and rolling stock. One positive aspect of the GNR's final demise was that all suburban passenger, main line passenger and rail freight services in the Dublin area were now under the control of one operator, CIE. It was now conceivable that a through suburban service could be operated between Howth and Bray or even Drogheda and Arklow, as eventually was the case.

The 1960s was not a positive decade for Dublin's railways however. Private car ownership continued to erode suburban rail traffic and the government and CIE even considered replacing the remaining suburban rail services with buses. On the main lines things were fairly stagnant in terms of development although some new modern coaches were acquired, notably the Cravens coaches assembled at Inchicore which still remain in service today almost forty years later. Freight services in the main were still being operated with the traditional four-wheeled loose-coupled wagons although this would soon change.

Fortunately suburban rail services survived and as private car numbers grew exponentially, Dublin started to slowly get strangled by traffic gridlock. In the remaining areas still served by suburban trains passenger numbers started to grow despite the appaling antiquity and unreliability of most of the stock available for these services. On the main lines passenger numbers started an upward trend that still thankfully continues today. One problem in this area in the 1960s and indeed through to comparatively recent times was that whilst passenger numbers were rising, the amount of available rolling stock was falling and ageing. A start at redressing this problem was the introduction from 1972 of air conditioned coaches designed and part-built by British Rail Engineering Limited with finishing work carried out by Inchicore works. The introduction of new rolling stock also allowed a new more intensive timetable to be operated on main line services. The cross border line from Connolly station (formerly Amiens Street) to Belfast also benefited from the introduction of modern rolling stock with the advent of Northern Ireland Railways new Enterprise sets.

Unfortunately for suburban passengers, the wait for decent rolling stock was to be somewhat longer than on the main lines. Recognising that Dublin's traffic was by now a very serious problem, various studies had been conducted by CIE and the government, into possible solutions to the traffic problem. One of the most promising of these was carried out by A M Voorhees into the creation of a rapid rail system and busway network for the capital including a central bus and underground station. Unfortunately at the this time in the 1970s there was a lack of political will to spend exchequer funds on such a project. Finally in 1979 the government of the day gave the green light for the first phase of the rapid rail project, the electrification of the Howth to Bray route, later to be known by its marketing name, Dublin Area Rapid Transit, or DART.

Whilst the electrification project was taking place another not insignificant extension to suburban passenger services took place. The year 1981 witnessed the introduction of a limited diesel-operated suburban service from Connolly station to Maynooth, serving Ashtown, Clonsilla, Leixlip (Louisa Bridge) and Maynooth. Lucan North had originally been included in the plan but was dropped along the way. Unlike the DART, which was an almost immediate success when it opened in 1984, the Maynooth service was very slow to build up passenger numbers. Rolling stock shortages and the antiquity of the stock used did not help the marketing of the service, but eventually passenger numbers grew. A further four stations were opened in 1990 and with the introduction of new diesel multiple units in 1994, the service began an enormous expansion which even saw the introduction of a set second set of rails between Clonsilla and Maynooth (singled by the GSR in 1931) and the operation of a limited Sunday service in 2001.

The DART service was an unparalleled success for Dublin's railways. Passenger numbers tripled in the first ten years of operation and the system was further extended to Greystones and Malahide, DART services to these places being introduced in 2001. New electric multiple units were also introduced at this time to add to the original fleet of 40 units. As a testimony to the success of the DART and those who operate it, despite a disastrous fire which ravaged Fairview DART depot in 2001 destroying a number of units and leaving only a third of the depot operational, an excellent service is still maintained seven days a week.

The Maynooth and DART services were not the only expansions and improvements to Dublin's rail system in recent years. The introduction of the aforementioned new diesel multiple units from 1994 onwards also allowed for the introduction of a brand new suburban service along the former Great Southern & Western route from Heuston to Kildare with new or re-opened stations en-route at Cherry Orchard, Clondalkin, Hazelhatch & Celbridge and Sallins & Naas. Like the old Midland line to Maynooth, a suburban service had never operated on this route hitherto. Unfortunately, Lucan was yet again left out as the former Lucan South station remains closed, despite the fact that Lucan is Dublin's fastest growing suburb, although a new station is planned for nearby Adamstown.

On the freight side, the nature of the traffic carried by Dublin's railways and the system as a whole, has changed greatly since the mid-1960s. The majority of the main commodities carried now did not exist in terms of rail traffic prior to that period. These include, cement, ores, ammonia and palletised fertiliser. The traditional four wheeled wagon had virtually disappeared by the end of the 1970s, as had cattle traffic, once a major source of income for the railways. Finally sundries traffic ended after a long slow decline. As a result of all these changes and the arrival of the concept of a one-customer block train, the need for sidings and shunting locomotives was drastically reduced. Containers, palletised loads, specialised wagons, gantries and forklifts had become the means by which freight traffic is expedited.

The latest developments in rail transport in Dublin's are perhaps the most far reaching. Almost six decades after the demise of CIE's last tram in 1949, and almost five decades after the closure of the Harcourt Street line, Dublin is about to get a modern successor to both, the LUAS light rail system. Line A of the LUAS will link Tallaght with the city centre at Middle Abbey Street. This will also be Tallaght's first rail link to the city since the demise of the Dublin & Blessington Tramway in 1932. A depot for servicing the new trams has been constructed on a site adjacent to the Red Cow in Clondalkin. The opening of this line is publicly scheduled for mid-2003.

Line B of the LUAS is also underway. This will connect the now enormous Sandyford Industrial Estate with the city centre near Stephen's Green. A possible future extension will take this line underground to Broadstone and beyond when and if it is later converted to a Metro line. The course of this line from the Sandyford to the Grand Canal will be along the trackbed of the former Harcourt Street line some of whose dismantled bridges have had to be rebuilt such as those at Taney Road and Dundrum as well as the Charlemont Street bridge over the Grand Canal.

Further lines are also planned. Line C will link Connolly Station and the adjacent International Services Centre with the Tallaght line at Middle Abbey Street. A fourth line, Line D, is also on the drawing board and

is proposed to connect the city centre with Ballymun and Dublin Airport which is one of the last non-rail connected major airports in Europe.

As if all of this railway revival is not enough, not only is the quadrupling of the present double track south-western main line from Inchicore to Hazelhatch & Celbridge on the cards, but there are very real prospects for the building of a comprehensive Metro system for the city. Not since their origin in the nineteenth century, has the future for the railways of Dublin, looked so bright.

## Acknowledgments

A book such as this could not be published without the contributions and assistance of a large number of people. To start with, the project would not have come to pass were it not for my good friend Des McGlynn and of course Tom Ferris, that champion of the written word on Irish railways. A special mention must also go to a number of individuals in Iarnrod Eireann, notably Barry Kenny, Kevin Forde, Gerry Tully, Liam Brennan, Brian Lucas and many others for their invaluable assistance and courtesy. Staff at two other state transport bodies, the Dublin Transportation Office and the Railway Procurement Agency were most help-ful, most notably Ciaron Mac Samhrain and Eamon Brady. Thanks are also due to staff at the National Photographic Archive and the Guinness archive, in particular Clare Hackett of the latter, who sourced a number of excellent photographs.

Aside from the organisations mentioned above, individuals who provided invaluable assistance, whether in generating leads or in actually supplying material included; Bernard C Byrne, John Cleary, Desmond Coakham, Brendan Duffner, Clifton Flewitt, Peter Jones, Michael Kennedy, Sean Kennedy, Michael Lalor, Robin Linsley of the Irish Railway Record Society's London area, Richard Murray, Robert Noblett, Gerry and Jackie O'Kelly, Alan O'Rourke, Alan Roome and Joe St. Leger. If I have inadvertently left anyone out, please accept my wholehearted apology.

Finally a mention must go to the staff at Midland Publishing and last but certainly not least to my wife Paula and son Cillian for putting up with my hobby and encouraging me to complete this book.

Below: **Kingsbridge was at one time an important location for the handling of rail freight. The stiff gradient out of the station to this day, tests the pulling power of locomotives and so it is no surprise to see Woolwich Mogul No. 383 steaming hard with its loose-coupled freight as it heads south-west out of the station on the main line in this early 1950s view.** Seán Kennedy

# KINGSBRIDGE TO KILDARE

Below: The Great Southern & Western Railway had reached Carlow in 1846 and Cork by 1849. It continued expanding to become the largest railway company in Ireland by the time of the 1925 amalgamation. This late 1970s aerial view of Kingsbridge terminus (by then known as Heuston), clearly illustrates the proportions of Sancton Wood's GSWR headquarters building and the adjoining train shed designed by Sir John McNeill. As was common in the Victorian era, the train shed contained an arrival and departure platform with carriage sidings in between, an arrangement that by the 1970s had become far too restrictive for the increasing passenger traffic. In December 1972, one of the centre carriage sidings was removed and a new double-faced platform was constructed, capable of handling a nine-coach train on either side. In conjunction with platform 1, the former 'military platform' (visible in the top left of the photograph), the number of platforms was increased to five in total. In the new millennium, passenger traffic has increased to such an extent that the number of platforms is being increased to nine. Three of these, Nos 6 to 8 are in an area formerly occupied by carriage storage sidings and a section of the car-park, itself the former goods yard. A ninth platform, ironically numbered platform 10, is located on the Islandbridge line, so far from the concourse that passengers had to be transferred there by bus, during the re-construction programme.
CIE/Iarnród Éireann

Above: **The station took its name from the adjacent cast iron bridge over the Liffey, which was opened in 1821. In recent years it was subject to a 2 tonne weight limit that prevented buses from using the bridge. In the early 1980s a new bridge was built almost parallel in conjunction with the re-routing of traffic along the quays. Presently, Kingsbridge, renamed Sean Heuston Bridge in 1966, after the Irish patriot, is being strengthened to take the LUAS light rail line A across the River Liffey.** Ian Allan Library

Right: **Up to the early 1950s many of the secondary expresses and stopping trains departing from Kingsbridge looked much as they had done in the GSWR era. Here D12 class 4-4-0 No 306 sets off for Kilkenny, with a train of ex-GSWR carriages.** Seán Kennedy

Above: **In 1939, the GSR's Inchicore works, turned out the three finest and most powerful steam locomotives ever to grace Ireland's railways. Built to the design of E C Bredin, the Chief Mechanical Engineer of the GSR, the 800 class locomotives (GSR class B1a), were restricted to the Cork line because of their weight. They handled the main Cork expresses until displaced by** diesels in the 1950s. This early CIE era view, circa 1948, shows No 801 *Macha* about to leave Kingsbridge on a Cork express. In the background the former goods offices, part of which today are occupied by the Irish Railway Record Society, are visible. Ian Allan Library

Below: **Ex-GSWR 4-6-0 locomotives of the 400 and 500 classes also handled top-link expresses out of Kingsbridge. When No 409 was photographed at the departure platform in Kingsbridge on the 27th May 1955, the station itself only boasted three platforms, something that would be an operational nightmare nowadays.** SLS collection

Right: **Moving on to this June 1986 view, steam-hauled trains had long vanished from Kingsbridge, a name itself unfamiliar to a new generation. In common with other major stations in the Irish Republic, it was renamed in 1966, after one of the leaders of the 1916 Rebellion. By 1986 Heuston as it had become, reverberated to the sound of General Motors engines such as 141 class No 170, on pilot duties, and the 071 class locomotive behind.** Dónal Murray

Below: **By the early 1990s, Iarnród Éireann desperately needed new locos. Salvation came in 1994 in the form of the 201 class built in Canada by General Motors. Including the two acquired by Northern Ireland Railways to work the Belfast to Dublin expresses jointly with IE, 34 locomotives were delivered. By 1997, when this view of No 227, on a morning Cork express, was taken, the 201 class dominated almost all top link services.** John Cleary

Above: **In 1936, the GSR completely modernised the signalling system in a number of locations around Dublin including Kingsbridge. In 2002 this was outdated and needed replacement. Complete resignalling of the area was undertaken in conjunction with the rebuilding of the station. With only months to go until its removal, the rear of the GSR built cabin is seen here from the valeting plant roads.** Dónal Murray

Above: **Operating 24 hours a day, maintaining and cleaning coaching stock, Heuston's valeting plant has been a constantly busy place since its construction in the 1970s. On a cold February day in 2002, 141 class No 171 propels a Mk1 Generating Steam Van and a short rake of Cravens coaches out of the plant towards the station platforms.** Dónal Murray

Below: **An exterior view of the valeting plant. Just visible behind the Mk 3 van to the right of the locomotive, is part of the carriage wash plant. To the left, several sidings have already been removed in preparation for the station's expansion.** Dónal Murray

Above: **The 141 class GMs have given exemplary performance on Irish railways for almost 40 years. When less than a decade old, and bearing its original number, B176 hauls an up Cork express into Heuston in the late 1960s. The driver is wearing a cap with a white top as this train is quite a distinguished express called the 'Seandún'. Making only one stop at Limerick Junction, this train left Cork at 08.10 and is seen arriving in the capital at 11:00am.** Bernard C Byrne

Above right: **The GSR colour light signalling system of the 1930s, which was very sophisticated for the period, was upgraded in a piecemeal fashion over the years. Here, a modern route indicator has been added under this two-aspect 1930s colour light signal. Increasing traffic levels and the age of the equipment, were the factors leading to its replacement in 2002.**
Dónal Murray

Below: **In complete contrast to the 'Seandún' and almost 30 years later, 201 class No 217 eases into platform 5, the former arrivals platform, with an up Cork train in 1995. Visible behind the third and fourth Mk 2 coaches is the former Guinness sidings gantry erected in 1969 and capable of lifting 25 tons. In later years the gantry was little used except for some permanent way trains. It was dismantled by February 2002.** Des McGlynn

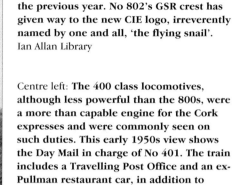

Left: **Making a typically dramatic exit from Kingsbridge, No 802 *Tailte*, blasts up the grade out of the station with the 10.00am express to Cork and Tralee, in June 1946. Several vehicles of this train have been repainted in the livery of CIE, formed only the previous year. No 802's GSR crest has given way to the new CIE logo, irreverently named by one and all, 'the flying snail'.**
Ian Allan Library

Centre left: **The 400 class locomotives, although less powerful than the 800s, were a more than capable engine for the Cork expresses and were commonly seen on such duties. This early 1950s view shows the Day Mail in charge of No 401. The train includes a Travelling Post Office and an ex-Pullman restaurant car, in addition to some GSR steel-panelled coaches.**
Seán Kennedy

Below: **No. 800 *Maedhbh* is seen easing her way into Kingsbridge in very early CIE days with a long express from Cork. Steam has evidently been shut off as the locomotive coasts towards the arrival platform. The GSR crest is still visible on No 800's tender although the 'GS' initials are gone and the second ex-GSWR coach is repainted in CIE's original two-tone green livery. It is notable that the only modern looking coach in the train is a 1935 Bredin vehicle which is possibly the unique all-First Class No 1144. Some of the colour light signals dating from the 1936 re-signalling scheme are also clearly evident in this view.**
Seán Kennedy

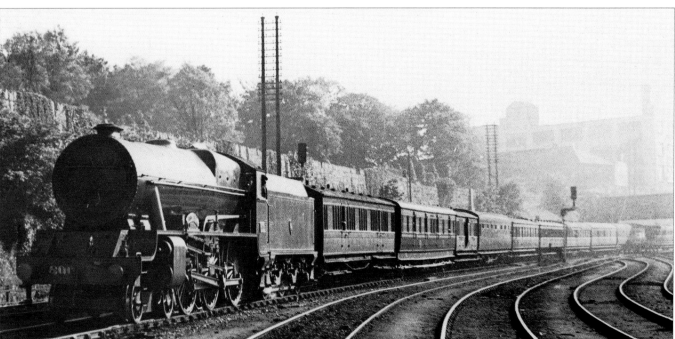

## INCHICORE SHED

Above: **Inchicore's running shed was, and still is, the busiest depot in the entire country. In September 1951, the former GSWR depot was still steam dominated and No 327, a Coey designed and Inchicore built 4-4-0 of GSR class D2, is seen here, still going strong, being prepared for service some half of a century after it was built at the adjacent works.** Ian Allan Library

Centre right: **Following 'The Emergency' as the Second World War was known in neutral Éire, the railways were just beginning to return to normal when the severe winter of 1947 completely disrupted coal imports from the UK. The railways again struggled to operate and a number of locomotives were converted temporarily to oil burning such as Woolwich Mogul, No 397 of GSR class K1a, seen here in March 1947. The white painted circles on the smokebox and the tender denoted that she was an oil burner.** SLS collection

Bottom right: **In 1947, CIE and the GNR introduced a new through train, from Belfast to Cork via Dublin. Coaching stock was provided by both companies and the trains were hauled by GNR 4-4-0s between Belfast and Dublin and CIE 4-6-0s from Dublin to Cork. No 800 *Maedhbh* is seen here being readied for this service in 1948, at the Inchicore running shed.**
Courtesy, Iarnród Éireann

Top: **The views on this page lead us out of the city and down the GSWR main line. Approaching Inchicore from Kingsbridge in April 1948 with a rake of open wagons, is No 360 of the GSR class K3, a Coey designed locomotive of 1903 vintage. The engine, displays the white discs also seen on No 397 on the previous page, which informed signalmen and running staff alike that the locomotive was an oil-burner and was therefore to be given priority. All locomotives converted to oil burning reverted to coal once supplies normalised. The experiment, or rather the expedient, of oil burning, which was also tried in Britain at around the same time, was clearly not a great success.**
SLS collection

Centre: **The area to the west of Inchicore has greatly changed since the 1950s with the spread of suburban housing. On 9th June 1956 a three-car diesel set hauling a six-wheeled van approaches Inchicore on the 8.15am Kilkenny to Dublin service.**
N. W. Sprinks

Bottom: **Until 1947 a station existed between Clondalkin and Hazelhatch called Lucan South. Situated in excess of a mile from picturesque Lucan village, the station saw little use in its later years and was the earliest one to close on this section of line. Indeed in this 1988 view, as an 071 class hauled, Mk 3 set speeds south out of the city, the surrounding area had yet to be built up. Today this view is completely unrecognisable, particularly on the left hand side of the tracks where the author's house is just one of many hundreds.**
Dónal Murray

## CLONDALKIN

Below: **Like the 800s, there were only three class B1 4-6-0s. Designed by Bazin and built by Inchicore works between 1924 and 1926, these powerful locomotives mainly worked on the Cork main line prior to dieselisation. No 502, passes Clondalkin** station in the late 1940s, coasting towards Kingsbridge with an express whose leading vehicle is of one of the magnificent twelve-wheel clerestories built by the GSWR for the Rosslare boat trains in 1903. Clondalkin station was closed in 1947 but reopened again in 1994. Seán Kennedy

Bottom: **In the same period as the previous photograph but on a brighter summer's day, a Coey 2-6-0 drifts through Clondalkin with a Cork to Kingsbridge goods train. These locomotives were originally designed as 0-6-0s but a leading pair of wheels was added due to excessive head-end weight.** Seán Kennedy

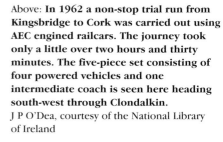

Above: **In 1962 a non-stop trial run from Kingsbridge to Cork was carried out using AEC engined railcars. The journey took only a little over two hours and thirty minutes. The five-piece set consisting of four powered vehicles and one intermediate coach is seen here heading south-west through Clondalkin.**
J P O'Dea, courtesy of the National Library of Ireland

Centre left: **Forty years later, railcars are once again regular visitors to Clondalkin station. Re-opened in 1994 and served by the commuter services to and from Kildare, which were originally operated by the 2600 class railcars, these workings now also see the latest 2700/2750 railcars. Here a three-coach unit formed of a two-car 2700 class set and one double-ended 2750 class unit arrives on a lunch-time service from Kildare to Heuston in February 2002.**
Dónal Murray

Bottom left: **Looking towards Heuston, the same train departs from Clondalkin under the bridge visible in J P O'Dea's photograph at the top of the page.**
Dónal Murray

## HAZELHATCH

Right: **Hazelhatch like Clondalkin, was closed from 1974 until 1994. Prior to closure, it handled a considerable volume of cattle traffic for a nearby meat processing plant. Often locomotives which had undergone repairs at Inchicore were taken out to Hazelhatch on test runs. In this 1962 view the loco concerned was a unique one, the solitary example of MAK traction in Ireland, No K801. Originally purchased by the GNRB for £27,500 in 1954 and numbered 800, the MAK as it was known, passed to CIE in 1958 when the GNRB was dissolved. It didn't see a great deal of use on the CIE system and spent its later years in the yard at Inchicore works before being sold to the Galway Metal Co. at Oranmore as a mobile generator where**

it remained, albeit partially dismantled, until relatively recently. J P O'Dea, courtesy of the National Library of Ireland

Above: **Steam hauled pick-up goods trains were at the very end of their days when this photograph was taken at Hazelhatch's goods shed in 1962, with 0-6-0 No 360, in charge of a light load.** J P O'Dea, courtesy of the National Library of Ireland

Right: **Ireland doesn't get much snow, compared to mainland Europe. In February 1986, Hazelhatch, amongst other places, was covered in snow creating this attractive scene as 081 speeds through the then closed station en-route from Cork to Dublin.** Ian Allan Library

Left: **In common with all of the other stations that were reopened in the 1990s for commuter traffic into the city, Hazelhatch was extensively rebuilt and improved. Platforms were raised, the footbridge was restored and the station building was given a facelift. With both the 2600 class railcar and station looking like they were 'straight out of the box', Hazelhatch & Celbridge as it was renamed, looked quite a picture in this May 1994 photograph.** Iarnród Éireann

## SALLINS

Centre: **At one time the mail train on any railway was probably be considered one of the more prestigious workings as speed was of the essence. Fast timings were often demanded by the postal authorities. The Cork to Dublin Day Mail was no exception and to maintain its schedule with limited stopping, it picked up mail en-route as well as at the terminal stations and some intermediate points. In this July 1951 view, the mail train is recorded just as it is about to pick up a sack of mail from the lineside apparatus, just outside Sallins. No 403 is the locomotive in charge of the train.** Ian Allan Library

Left: **Sallins, as well as being an inter-mediate station on the GSWR main line, was also the junction for the GSWR's long branch to Tullow. This line opened in stages in 1885 and 1886. The distance from Sallins to Tullow was 34¾ miles. Passenger trains on the branch were suspended in 1944 due to wartime shortages of coal. They were resumed briefly after the war but all regular passenger and goods services on the branch were withdrawn in 1947. Occasional livestock specials were run between then and April 1959, when CIE closed the line completely. In this June 1939 view, carriages for the branch have been detached from a main line train at Sallins.** SLS collection

## KILDARE

Top right: **Between Newbridge, the next station south after Sallins, and Kildare, trains pass through a place known around the world. The Curragh is the location for one of Ireland's most famous race-courses and is also the main training ground for the Irish Defence Forces. The Curragh has a basic station opened only on race days. At one time a short branch from the racecourse trailed in on the down side behind the photographer, but this was removed in the 1970s. On a cold February morning in 2002, a fertiliser special trundles through behind locomotive No 232.** Dónal Murray

Centre right: **Kildare has evolved over the years from a reasonably busy county town to a bustling commuter base for many working in Dublin. Located some 30 miles from the city, a substantial number of people commute to the capital each day. Waiting to take some of those commuters to Dublin, a 2750/2700 class set stands at the up platform in February 2002. In the centre lies a through road allowing non-stopping expresses and freights to by-pass standing trains. In fact, traffic on this portion of the Cork main line has expanded to such a degree that quadrupling of the track at the Dublin end of the line is being seriously discussed.** Dónal Murray

Bottom right: **We conclude our look at Kildare with a view inside the new civil engineering department plant depot which has been built there. For many years the plant depot was located inside the former DSER Barrow Street (formerly Grand Canal Street) running shed. When a new DART station was planned for the Barrow Street site, the plant depot was relocated to a brand new purpose-built facility at Kildare, located in the former goods yard there. A track inspection car manufactured by Matisa, on the right, and a Plasser 08-16 tamping and lining machine on the left, are being serviced in this February 2002 view.** Dónal Murray

Above: **Linking the GSWR to Dublin's other railways, the North Wall branch diverged on the up side just outside Kingsbridge, crossing the Liffey and tunnelling under the Phoenix Park. In early CIE days No 501 has crossed the Liffey bridge, while its train is still emerging from the Phoenix Park tunnel.** Seán Kennedy

Centre left: **Just north of the tunnel were Cabra cattle sidings. In 1965 bulk cement traffic replaced cattle here, until the late 1990s when the depot closed. The silos and cattle bank were to the left. In this June 1972 view, a liner train passes through en-route from the North Wall to Cork.**

Left: **Beyond Cabra, the GSWR trains originally joined the MGWR North Wall branch at Glasnevin Junction. In 1901, the GSWR opened its own route to the North Wall, seen here, trailing in from Kingsbridge, on the left. On the right the MGWR's branch to the North Wall disappears into a cutting and under a bridge. The connecting line in the centre right foreground was installed by the GSR in 1936 to enable MGWR line trains to be diverted to Westland Row. Originally this connection was the other way around, from the GSWR's Kingsbridge line to the MGWR North Wall branch. In the distance, in the upper right, some wagons can be seen at North City Mills, a short branch off the MGWR line.** Both, Bernard C Byrne

# FROM CATTLE TO COMMUTERS

## BROADSTONE

Right: **Broadstone was the Dublin terminus of MGWR line trains until 1937, when they were diverted to Westland Row. The MGWR works, engine shed and goods depot were also here. In this early 1930s view, an ex-MGWR 4-4-0, now GSR class D6 No 544, is at the station.** Midland Publishing collection

Below: **The MGWR's fine headquarters building was designed by J S Mulvany. After closure to passengers in 1937, Broadstone remained open as a locomotive depot for over another 20 years and is used today by Bus Éireann, the national bus company.** Iarnród Éireann

Left: **The track bed from Broadstone to Liffey Junction has lain derelict for almost 40 years now as is well illustrated by this view from the North Circular Road overbridge. However, it is just possible that in the not too distant future a double-track metro line may be built in this very location.** Dónal Murray

Below: **At the rear of Broadstone depot in steam days, coaling staithes existed complete with a travelling steam crane on broader than broad gauge tracks. In this photograph taken in the final years of operation, a motley collection of wagons is visible having disgorged their coal to power the last remaining steam locomotives.** J P O'Dea courtesy National Library of Ireland

Bottom: **Cattle traffic was the lifeblood of the MGWR and many of its numerous classes of engine were naturally built with this in mind. No 626 of GSR class J5 was a member of the most powerful class of MGWR goods locomotives. Built in 1924 at Broadstone and surviving almost to the end of steam, No 626, like the rest of its class also worked passenger trains for which their 5ft 8in driving wheels were most suited.** Des McGlynn collection

## LIFFEY JUNCTION

Right: **Liffey Junction, the first station out from Broadstone, was never much more than a transfer point for passengers except for one weekend in May 1972 when it served terminating trains from the west due to work at Connolly station. It was however an extremely important location for cattle trains as the Dublin cattle markets were located nearby. The MGWR branch to the North Wall diverged from the main line to Broadstone at Liffey Junction. When this photograph was taken in the early 1970s, cattle traffic was already finished on CIE's railways and the days of the pick-up and transfer goods such as this one were also numbered.** Bernard C Byrne

Centre right: **In the years following the demise of the cattle trains and with loose coupled goods stock gradually being withdrawn, the sidings at Liffey Junction became home to many wagons waiting scrapping, as seen here in July 1967.**

Below: **By 1994 the only significant structure left at Liffey Junction from its former glory days was the MGWR water tower. The commuters on the brand new 2600 class Arrow unit, had replaced the cattle, as the lifeblood of this section of the former MGWR.** Both, Des McGlynn

Left: **In 1990 four completely new stations were opened on the former Midland line between Connolly and Maynooth. One of these was Coolmine located between the former Blanchardstown station and Clonsilla. Rebuilt again in 2000 as part of the Maynooth line improvement, Coolmine plays host in this photograph to another new breed of commuter railcars, the 2800 class.** Dónal Murray

Centre left: **When the Maynooth section acquired its new suburban service in 1981, Clonsilla station was amongst those re-opened. Apart from the addition of a second-hand ex-DSER footbridge, from which the photograph was taken, this 1987 view looking towards Dublin, has scarcely changed from steam days. The former cattle loading docks, a feature of so many MGWR stations can still be seen.**
Dónal Murray

Below: **The station, seen in March 2002, has changed considerably. The old station buildings and semaphore signals are gone, replaced by a standard design metal clad building, colour light signals and a signal relay room, to the right of the picture, beyond the level crossing. Only the signal cabin, retained to work the wooden crossing gates remains as before, though this would not last for much longer either.**
Dónal Murray

Above: **Like Coolmine, Leixlip Confey was a new station in 1990. Upon opening it had only one platform and one running line together with a converted container which was used as a ticket office. In this April 2002 view, a 2800 Class railcar departs from the newly rebuilt Confey station en-route to Maynooth. The station now boasts two platforms, two running lines and a new station building in the standard style for this route.** Dónal Murray

Centre right: **Lucan North had ceased to be a passenger station as far back as 1941. No longer in railway ownership, the station remained in more or less original condition, including the shelter on the down platform, in this 1988 view. It had been proposed to re-open the station in 1981 but this did not materialise.**
Dónal Murray

Right: **Bizarrely, Lucan is still without a railway station in 2002 despite being the fastest growing Dublin suburb. The station building has now been transformed beyond recognition by its present owners and one very positive thing is the appearance of a second running line, absent since 1931.**
Dónal Murray

Above: **In MGWR, GSR and CIE days, Leixlip only had one station. This was and still is located at Louisa Bridge, somewhat more remote from the centre of the village than the much newer Confey station. Seen here circa 1950, complete with single line staff snatching apparatus visible between the main line and the cattle siding, Leixlip closed in 1963 only to re-open again in 1981 and then be completely transformed by 2002.** Seán Kennedy

Centre left: **When suburban services to Maynooth re-opened in 1981, CIE had barely enough resources to cobble together a service of any kind. Shortly after the re-opening that year, 001 class 052 is seen hauling a five-piece push-pull set, a bizarre combination indeed. These clapped out trains did nothing to stimulate traffic and it was only with the arrival of the new railcars in 1994 that serious improvements to the service began to pay dividends in terms of increased passenger numbers.** Ian Allan Library

Left: **The reconstruction of the Maynooth section and reinstatement of double track on this part of the former MGWR line, at the beginning of the new millennium, reflected a political imperative to get commuters onto the trains and off Dublin's seriously overcrowded roads. In this scene a new crossover is being lifted into position by a crane beyond the wall to the left of the picture whilst a rail-mounted Atlas excavator carries out other work.** Iarnród Éireann

Right and centre right: **The next station west of Maynooth was Kilcock. Closed in 1963, the station building at Kilcock is now a private residence. Its appearance has hardly changed over nearly 40 years except for the absence of the loop and the growth of the vegetation. A new station situated more conveniently to the village centre was opened recently.** Author's collection and Dónal Murray

Below: **Enfield, is as far to the west of the city, as we are going on this pictorial journey. Like Kilcock, the station was closed in 1963. It was however reopened in 1988 with a limited morning and evening week-day service being provided. In May 1993, Enfield was host to a Railway Preservation Society of Ireland special hauled by the preserved ex DSER 2-6-0 No 461, built in 1922. The locomotive is seen here running around its train in preparation for the journey back to Maynooth and Connolly. Enfield's goods shed and lengthy cattle dock are still evident long after the end of goods services.** Dónal Murray

## THE DUBLIN & MEATH LINE

Above left: **The former MGWR line from Clonsilla Junction to Navan closed to all traffic in 1963. In 1964, ex-GNR railcar A, or at least the remains of it, was engaged in track lifting operations near Bective. This was the GNR's pioneering diesel railcar built at Dundalk works in 1932. It was earmarked for preservation before being** badly damaged in a collision. Its last days were spent in the hands of a Donegal-based contractor who dismantled redundant railways. Ian Allan Library

Above right: **Kilmessan, situated south of Bective, was the junction for the Athboy branch. Much of the station and the signal cabin survive today.** Dónal Murray

Below: **At Navan Junction, the MGWR line from Clonsilla to Kingscourt crossed the** GNR line from Drogheda to Oldcastle. Nothing remains of this station today except the old goods store. The line to Clonsilla Junction on the right, has been gone for nearly 40 years but a single line of rails still exist where the GNR train is seen, serving Tara Mines and Kingscourt. In late 2002 there were no scheduled freight services to either location but where the track survives, there is always the hope that both freight and passenger traffic may someday return. SLS collection

# GOD'S NORTHERN RAILWAY

## THE NAVAN BRANCH

Above: **We commence our journey on the tracks of the former Great Northern Railway at Navan station. The 17 mile long line from Drogheda to Navan opened in 1850 and was extended to Oldcastle in 1863. Though passenger services ended in 1958, Navan retained goods traffic until 1982. Also from 1977, freight trains served the nearby Tara Zinc Mines, a short distance up the former Oldcastle branch and gypsum trains ran on the former MGWR line to Kingscourt. Framed nicely by GNR semaphore signals in this early 1990s view, an 071 class awaits the road with a Tara Mines-bound empty ore train.** Des McGlynn

Right: **In 1984, C class No 222 passes through the disused Beauparc station, between Navan and Drogheda, with a set of gypsum hoppers.** A J O'Rourke.

## DROGHEDA

Left: **Moving on to Drogheda, a town which has been home to two cement factories, we take a look at the original one located adjacent to the River Boyne with the impressive viaduct carrying the Belfast to Dublin main line visible in the centre background in this 1950s view. Cement provided an important source of traffic for the GNR and later CIE and Iarnród Éireann. This factory closed in the 1970s, the factory at Platin on the Navan branch became the sole manufacturer of cement in this area.** Courtesy of Duffners

Below: **Drogheda's main line station situated immediately south of the magnificent Boyne viaduct has always been a hive of activity. It was no exception when this photograph was taken in the 1950s as a GNR AEC railcar rounds the curve into the station with the south bound 'Enterprise'. These railcars brought a whole**

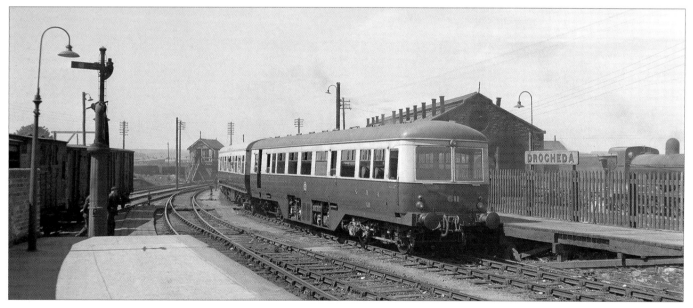

**new standard of comfort and efficiency to the GNR's international main line.**
Desmond Coakham

Left: **Whilst the AEC railcars were a sign of what was to come, they were actually built only two years after the last Great Northern steam locomotives, the elegant VS class 4-4-0s, which entered service in 1948. One of these locomotives, in the beautiful GNR blue livery and hauling a rake of the immaculate teak liveried coaches, enters Drogheda station from the south on a Belfast express.** Desmond Coakham

Top: **After an absence of many years, railcars again returned to Drogheda in the 1990s with the advent of the Japanese built Mitsui 2600 class and later the Spanish Alstom built 2700 class. A trial train of the latter units is seen here in 1998. The station has been rebuilt to cater for the burgeoning commuter traffic between Drogheda and Dublin and a new railcar** depot is being built to service the vehicles used on these trains. Iarnród Éireann.

Above: **Just beyond the end of the platforms, the line curves sharply to cross the River Boyne on a high viaduct, which is one of the wonders of the Irish railway network. Originally built in the 1850s, the viaduct was extensively renewed and** strengthened by the GNR in the 1930s. Here, a 181 class locomotive is easing its way across the bridge with a southbound 'Enterprise' working. The harsh winter sunlight gives atmosphere to this 1970 scene. Bernard C Byrne

Left: **Locomotive-hauled outer suburban trains may soon be a thing of the past in the Dublin area as the new railcars take over more and more services, but they were still the norm in 1984 as C class No 209 hauled its consist of 1950s Park Royal, CIE-built coaches and an ex-BR heating van into Laytown.** A J O'Rourke

Centre left: **When Butlins opened a holiday camp at Mosney in 1948 the GNR built a single platform station for it on a loop off the main line. By 1995 Mosney was in its twilight years as a holiday centre, but certain trains still called there during the summer, such as this 201 hauled Mk 2 set, forming a south bound 'Enterprise' service.** Dónal Murray

Below: **The mid-1990s saw a massive capital injection of European Union and government funding into the cross-border route, both in terms of infrastructure and rolling stock. The former GNR main line was completely re-laid and resignalled with work very much in evidence in this view of Gormanston. The signal cabin was later removed and now resides at the Cavan & Leitrim Railway's Dromod station.** Iarnród Éireann

## BALBRIGGAN

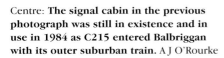

Top: **Balbriggan was almost completely burned down during the Irish War of Independence. The only thing burning in this 1950s view of the station is the coal inside the firebox of the GNR LQG class 0-6-0 No 112, as it heads south towards the capital with its long rake of vans.**
Des McGlynn collection

Centre: **The signal cabin in the previous photograph was still in existence and in use in 1984 as C215 entered Balbriggan with its outer suburban train.** A J O'Rourke

Bottom: **A little over ten years later and the new 201 class was on the scene. These super-powerful locomotives took over the numbers vacated by the Metropolitan Vickers C class engines built in 1956/57, which had all been withdrawn by 1986. The 201s are capable of handling the heaviest and fastest trains on the island such as the new 'Enterprise' sets built by De Dietrich in France in the 1990s. One of these trains is seen here at Balbriggan on a demonstration and publicity run just prior to the introduction of the new service.**
Iarnród Éireann

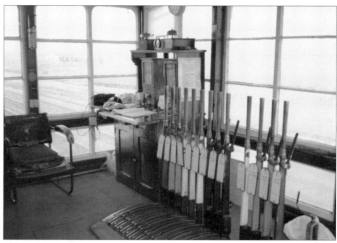

Above left and right: **By the time these photographs of Skerries signal cabin were taken in the early 1990s, the end of semaphore signalling on this route was nigh. The 14-lever McKenzie and Holland frame inside the cabin would soon be consigned to history.** Both Des McGlynn

Centre left: **The new generation of railcars are now undergoing their first livery change as is evidenced by this view of a 2600 class unit entering Rush & Lusk on a very damp Sunday 24th January 2002. The new 'Commuter' branded livery, whilst not to everyone's taste is certainly a welcome change from the previous unimaginative liveries.** Dónal Murray

Left: **Rush & Lusk was the scene of a potentially serious accident on 5th January 1963 when a UTA railcar set on a Belfast working derailed at the station. Fortunately no one was killed in the derailment. Work had already begun to clear the line by the time J P O'Dea arrived with his camera.** J P O'Dea courtesy of the National Library of Ireland

## MALAHIDE

Right: **The GNR and the DSER were the only pre-amalgamation railways serving Dublin that provided anything resembling a regular suburban service. On such a working, GNR T2 class 4-4-2 tank locomotive No 186, coasts across the Broadmeadows causeway just outside Malahide station.** Ian Allan Library

Centre right: **Malahide has always been one of north county Dublin's most picturesque towns. It has grown greatly in recent years, its popularity swelled by the train service into the heart of the city. Malahide was and is of course served by outer suburban services to Drogheda, but on the 9th October 2000, the DART too, finally arrived. Pictured here in January 2002 is one of the original Linke-Hofmann Busch built DART units, about to depart for another location recently added to the DART system, Greystones.** Dónal Murray

Below: **The DART extension to Malahide was still undergoing trials and driver route learning when this photograph was taken. The 2700 class railcar set on the left was also quite new.** Iarnród Éireann

## HOWTH JUNCTION

Above: Howth Junction is where the former GNR branch to the small harbour town of Howth leaves the Dublin to Belfast main line. Even in GNR days a healthy suburban

traffic existed and by 1972 CIE, the inheritors of this route, needed new trains to replace the ageing AEC railcars that were all but life-expired. As no funding was forthcoming, CIE converted old AEC railcars into four and five piece push-pull sets for use with the recently re-engined C201 class. Intended as a stop-gap measure

only, these units soldiered on, in an increasingly dilapidated condition, until the arrival of the new electric trains in the early 1980s. A generation of Dublin commuters will grimly remember, without a trace of nostalgia, the uncomfortable plastic seats in these units. On the 15th August 1973, driving trailer No 6102 is at the head of a push pull service from Howth as it leaves the branch to move on to the main line at Howth Junction.
Ian Allan Library

Left: With the impending introduction of the DART clearly marked by the presence of overhead line equipment and new signals, the days of the push-pull set seen here taking the Howth branch, and the adjacent signal cabin, were clearly numbered in this 1983 view. The introduction of the electric trains also heralded the end of the line for the C class diesels. No 209 was withdrawn in October 1984. CIE/Iarnród Éireann

Right: **Howth station itself still retains much of its original GNR architecture despite extensive rebuilding and the addition of a second platform for the introduction of the DART service in June 1984. The first week of operation of the new service was in the middle of a glorious heat wave and a new four-car DART unit basks in the sunlight as it awaits to return to Bray.** Joe St Leger

Centre right: **In complete contrast to the 1980s DART, this GNR T2 tank and its train of compartment stock is typical of what could be seen on the branch in the 1950s. GNR diesel railcars were also frequently used on the Howth services in those days. Children play on the wall behind where the second platform now exists.** SLS collection

Below: **Until the early 1970s only one intermediate station existed on the branch, that at Sutton, which was sometimes known as Sutton & Baldoyle. Sutton was the location of the depot for the GNR's electric tramway which ran from here, via Howth Head, to Howth station. The Hill of Howth Tramway closed in 1959 to be replaced by a bus service. One of the trams, in the GNR bus and railcar livery of blue and cream, may be seen to the right of the picture.** SLS collection

Left: **Back to the main line and nearing the Amiens Street terminus, we see former GNR VS class 4-4-0 No 210 *Erne*, renumbered 59 by its post 1958 owners, the Ulster Transport Authority, heading north up the bank through Killester with a train for Belfast.** SLS collection

Centre left: **The first station heading north out of the GNR terminus had been Clontarf. This was located north of the Clontarf Road and closed in 1956. In the new millennium a station, called Clontarf Road, was opened adjacent to the Fairview DART depot to serve Clontarf and the adjacent Eastpoint Business Park. A southbound DART is seen here at the new station.** Iarnród Éireann

Below: **By 1971 when this photo was taken, steam was long gone from regular services around Dublin. However, GNR steam locomotives had not entirely disappeared. S class 4-4-0 No 171 *Slieve Gullion*, was thankfully preserved by the Railway Preservation Society of Ireland when it was withdrawn by the UTA in the 1960s, and can still be seen on excursions to this day. Fairview railcar depot, on the left of the picture, and the surrounding area, have all changed radically since this photograph was taken. The water tower, semaphore signals and first generation rail cars have all gone and the shed was completely rebuilt to house the DART trains. The area to the right of No 171 has now been reclaimed from the sea and is totally unrecognisable.** Bernard C Byrne

## AMIENS STREET

Above: **Seen at the Amiens Street terminus of the GNR, is V class compound No 84**

*Falcon.* **Sister locomotive No 85** *Merlin,* **has been preserved, and occasionally visits its old haunt.**

Below: **In the early 1950s, when the 'Enterprise' ran through to Cork, CIE 800**

class 4-6-0s were regular visitors to Amiens Street. Here we see No 802 *Táilte* pulling into Amiens Street from Cork with the CIE set that includes an ex-Pullman restaurant car. A GNR. Locomotive will then take over for the journey north. Both, Seán Kennedy

Above: **In a photograph that evokes the atmosphere of a bygone era, GNR V class compound No 83 *Eagle* has arrived at the station to work the 5.30pm Dublin to Belfast 'Enterprise Express' on Monday 11th August 1947, the day this famous train ran for the first time** . Ian Allan Library

Below: **Moving on to 1970, Amiens Street was renamed Connolly in 1966, in honour of the Irish patriot and trade union leader, James Connolly. The UTA had thankfully come and gone and its successor NIR, had just acquired new rolling stock for the cross border services. Brand new Hunslet** diesel electric locomotive, No 102 *Falcon*, which entered traffic in July of that year, complete with 'Enterprise' headboard, stands at the buffers in Connolly with a train of Mk 2 stock, equipped for push-pull working. Ian Allan Library

Right: **Moving on another 27 years, Connolly station is as busy as ever. Here a pair of 121 class GMs haul a train of ammonia tankers off the loop line en-route from Marino Point in Cork to the Irish Fertilisers plant at Shelton Abbey near Arklow.** John Cleary

Centre right: **Since 1973 all Sligo trains have departed from Connolly. The motive power on this route is now almost universally the 071 class, these locomotives having been cascaded from busier routes with the delivery of the 201 class from 1994 onwards. On a bright summer's morning in 1996 one such No 082 prepares to depart for Sligo.** Des McGlynn

Below: **When the GSR closed the former MGWR Broadstone station in 1937, Midland line trains were re-routed through Amiens Street and via the loop line, to Westland Row. This brought a variety motive power to the GNR station. Here an express for Galway, headed by Woolwich Mogul No 373, passes through the loop line platforms at Amiens Street, at the start of its long journey to the west, in March 1954.** Ian Allan Library

Left: **We conclude our travels on the former GNR with these exterior and aerial views of Amiens Street station. The facade is little changed from that opened by the Dublin & Drogheda Railway in 1844, save for the addition of an escalator.**

Below: **This aerial view of Connolly station, taken in the late 1970s as construction work in connection with the electrification of the suburban services got underway, clearly illustrates the relationship between the former City of Dublin Junction Railway's loop line built in 1906 to link Amiens Street to Westland Row, and the original GNR terminus. Beyond the train shed covering the terminal platforms, may be seen Connolly's carriage valeting plant built in the 1970s and an extensive network of sidings in the former goods yard. If this view were to be taken today Connolly would look little different , though the surrounding area has been completely transformed with office developments.** Both, CIE/Iarnród Éireann

# SOUTH OF THE LIFFEY

Above: **With the opening of the CDJR loop line in 1891, Amiens Street was linked to the DSER's coastal route to Bray and beyond. When CIE took over the former GNR lines in the Republic in 1958 it became possible, thanks to the existence of this connection, to organise through suburban services between the northeastern and south-eastern suburbs. Framed nicely by the bridge to the loop line platforms that existed in pre-DART days, B184 prepares to depart with a Dalkey bound suburban service on the 10th June 1969.** Ian Allan Library

Right: **The GSR in its twenty-one year existence turned out only a handful of locomotive classes. One of these was the sole member of the P1 class, 2-6-2 tank, No 850, built in 1928. This locomotive spent most if its life on suburban services on the former DSER section and is seen here at the Amiens Street water tower in the early 1950s.** David Murray, courtesy Seán Kennedy

Above: **Immediately after crossing the bridge that spans the River Liffey, trains enter Tara Street, the only intermediate station on the former CDJR section. Another GSR built locomotive is seen here, circa 1950, in the form of class I3 0-6-2, No 671, one of a small class of tank locomotives built for suburban services. No 671 is hauling some of the carriages built in the 1930s by the GSR, for such services.** Courtesy, Seán Kennedy

Below left: **Tara Street nowadays, is the busiest station in the country handling 25,000 passengers each day. A major reconstruction is planned for the site involving a new station with facility for a proposed metro interchange at a later date. More significantly, the massive multi-storey retail and commercial complex, seen here in these interior and exterior artist's impressions of the project, are also planned for the site.** Iarnród Éireann

## WESTLAND ROW

Top left: **One of the initial objectors to the CDJR was Trinity College whose property the line traversed. Agreement between the parties was eventually reached and the line still crosses part of their property as is evidenced by this 1983 photograph of a DART unit on trial prior to the commencement of services the following year.** Ian Allan Library

Top right: **This is Westland Row station, former headquarters and terminus of Ireland's first railway the Dublin & Kingstown Railway, which opened in 1834. Seen here in the early-1970s, an escalator leads to the platforms and the floor is covered in the black and white tiles which appeared at the other main Dublin stations in this period. Westland Row was renamed Pearse station in 1966, after the leader of the 1916 rebellion.** Ian Allan Library

Above: **This 1960s panorama of the station interior illustrates Westland Row's function as a terminal and through station. The centre through-roads were created for the CDJR connection and today form an integral part of the DART and suburban system and of course the main line to Rosslare. The bay platforms that once served terminating DSER main line trains, continued in GSR and CIE days up to 1973, to handle main line trains to the west of Ireland over the former MGWR system.** Courtesy, Seán Kennedy

Above: **The photographs on this page cover a period of almost 50 years and illustrate three distinct generations of suburban trains. In the top photograph a former DSER tank loco No 428, GSR class F2, is seen arriving at Westland Row from the southern suburbs in June 1953. The colour light signals date from the GSR's 1936 resignalling scheme.** Ian Allan Library

Centre left: **More than a decade and a half later, an AEC railcar set departs from Westland Row heading south, the impressive overall roofs of the station are visible behind the railcars. Interestingly, this photograph was taken from the 1936 GSR-built signal cabin which was situated on a structure spanning the tracks. It survived until the line was electrified.** Bernard C Byrne

Bottom left: **Moving on to April 2002, steam and the first-generation of diesel railcars have long since disappeared. The first 8100/8300 class of DART electric multiple units took over inner suburban services on the Howth to Bray route in June 1984. Ten years later, outer and western suburban services benefited from the introduction of the Mitsui 2600 class diesel multiple units, an example of which is seen here in the new Commuter livery. These units are numbered in the same series as the first generation AEC railcars. A second generation of DART units is now being introduced with two types already in service, one of these, a Mitsui 8500 class unit, can be seen in the bay platform beside the diesel railcars.** Dónal Murray

## GRAND CANAL STREET

Top right: **Just south of Westland Row was the former DSER's Grand Canal Street depot and one time works. Grand Canal Street works had the distinction of being the first railway company works in the world to build its own locomotive. By the time this photograph of No 850 was taken in the 1950s, the works had been closed for almost a quarter of a century and all that remained was a locomotive depot.**
Ian Allan Library

Centre right: **At the end of Ireland's War of Independence in 1922, two 2-6-0 goods locomotives arrived for the DSER. These locomotives later became 461 and 462 of GSR's K2 class. No 462 is seen here at the Grand Canal Street shed awaiting its next turn of duty. Its sister No 461, has been preserved and is in the care of the Railway Preservation Society of Ireland.**
SLS collection

Bottom: **This lovely panorama of Grand Canal Street shed, taken in the late GSR period, is full of the atmosphere of the steam age. Over the following years the shed saw many different kinds of traction and machinery before ceasing to exist at the end of the twentieth century when a brand new station was built on the site. The last use that the shed was put to in the years prior to its demolition, was as a plant servicing depot for the Civil Engineering Department, a function now transferred to Kildare.** SLS collection

Top left: **As we leave the city and head south, our last look at Grand Canal Street depot shows a down Rosslare train hauled by 0-6-0 No 354, passing by on the main line in August 1948. As can be seen from the siding to the left of the train, six-wheel coaching stock was still quite common at this time. Many ex-GSWR carriages were drafted onto the former DSER section by the GSR after the Irish grouping in 1925, as the DSER lost the greatest number of vehicles in the troubles of the 1920s.** SLS collection

Centre: **As the city of Dublin has become more and more gridlocked, rail commuting where available has become more popular than ever. Passenger journeys on the DART have increased three-fold since 1984 and as was remarked earlier, new trains have been introduced recently to cope with the increased demand. The DART system itself has been extended at its northern and southern extremities to Malahide and Greystones. New stations have also been opened close to the city centre. We saw Clontarf Road earlier and this is its south side equivalent, Grand Canal Dock, opened at Barrow Street in January 2001. One of the new 8500 class DART electric units is seen on trial at the station.** Iarnród Éireann

Bottom: **One doesn't have to be a rail enthusiast or even a rail commuter to recognise this location as the venue of many international soccer and rugby matches. It is indeed fortunate that Landsdowne Road is next to the rail line and has its own station. In this view taken in April 1971, a south-bound service to Bray, hauled by A52r, one of the Metropolitan Vickers locos delivered in 1956 and rebuilt in 1969 with a General Motors engine, passes under the grandstand and enters Landsdowne Road station. Some elderly coaching stock was used on these services in the early 1970s, an ex-GSWR compartment coach is one of the vehicles in this set.** Ian Allan Library

Top: **Closed in 1960, Sandymount had to wait until June 1984 to see a passenger train stop again. On the day of its re-opening, a pair of DART units headed by 8320 arrive at the station.** Joe St. Leger

Below left: **The next station down the line is at Sydney Parade. It too closed in 1960 but re-opened in 1972. The first train into Sydney Parade on the re-opening day, 6th June 1972, was an AEC railcar set headed by 2635. Interestingly, the bridge that frames the railcar nicely in this photograph had previously been erected at Sandymount. CIE always seemed to make good use of redundant bridges.** Joe St Leger

Right: **A a push-pull set propelled by B219, a re-engined C class locomotive, is seen at the re-opened station.** Ian Allan Library

Below right: **On the other end of the southbound push-pull set propelled by B219 was control car, Driving Open Standard, No 6101. This had previously been AEC railcar No 2646, converted to push-pull working in 1972.**
Ian Allan Library

## STEAM SUBURBAN SERVICES

Above: **On these pages we will look at some of the motive power used on suburban services south of the Liffey in the era before the diesels and the DART. Earlier we** saw I3 class 0-6-2 No 671 at Tara Street station. Here another member of the class, No 674, is preparing to depart from Sydney Parade in the same period, the early 1950s. The leading coach in the train is one of the GSR built suburban coaches of the 1930s. Seán Kennedy

Below: **Moving on just a few years a J9 class 0-6-0 No 354, pulls into Sandymount with a southbound train. The train is passing under the footbridge that later ended up at Sydney Parade when it reopened in 1972.** SLS collection

Top: **One of the most versatile and certainly the most numerous steam locomotive class to have existed in Ireland was the ex-GSWR 101 class, which became the J15 class in GSR and CIE days. These 0-6-0 locomotives were built between 1866 and 1903 and two still exist today in preservation, Nos 184 and 186. In the 1950s, the J15s could turn up almost anywhere. They were really mixed traffic locomotives, as much at home on passenger as on goods trains. Two J15s are seen here in the southern suburbs powering this Wexford GAA special past Blackrock's Cloncurry Towers.**

Centre: **There should be no doubt in anyone's mind that Seán Kennedy is a brilliant photographer and this is perfectly exemplified by this magnificent photograph of the ubiquitous and sadly unique 2-6-2 tank, No 850, powering along the coast between Booterstown and Blackrock with a southbound suburban working.**

Below: **Near the same location and in the same period, ex-DSER 4-4-2 tank No 455 of GSR class C2 was also captured with a short south-bound suburban working.**
All photos on this page, Seán Kennedy

## DUN LAOGHAIRE & KILLINEY

Above left: **Carlisle Pier Dún Laoghaire was a place that the author and many others before him frequently stepped off the train and walked onto the mail boat for Holyhead. Looking almost lonely, A49r and its single van for the mail, awaits the road onto the main line off the short branch in August 1974. The last train called here in 1980 and now even the mail boat is gone.**
Ian Allan Library

Above right: **Until 1957, Dún Laoghaire, originally known as Kingstown, was a railway bottleneck as the double line from Westland Row narrowed to a single line between here and Dalkey. In that year, a second line of rails was introduced and Dún Laoghaire gained a new platform, seen here on its first day of use.**
Ian Allan Library

Left: **The 1957 layout remained until further reconstruction was required at Dún Laoghaire in preparation for the introduction of the DART services. This necessitated the rebuilding of the station and lowering of the track bed between Dún Laoghaire and Sandycove. A considerable amount of rock-breaking and the introduction of slab track was necessary to achieve the clearances required for the overhead wires. Suburban services were severely restricted during this operation. Here No 231 creeps out of the station with a southbound push-pull set whilst work proceeds on the up line's track bed, in the summer of 1981.** CIE/Iarnród Éireann

Above: **One of the most breathtaking views to be had in the Dublin area, comes as a train emerges from the darkness of the short Dalkey tunnel and the broad sweep of Killiney Bay unfolds. Hopefully some of the passengers on C218's push-pull set are savouring that view as they head towards Killiney station in 1980.** CIE/Iarnród Éireann

Right: **Creating plenty of dirty exhaust smoke and heading the other way nine years earlier, AEC-powered railcar No 2620 heads for Dalkey tunnel, Killiney Hill's obelisk being visible at the summit.**

Below: **Thankfully not creating as much smoke, No 2612 heads a main line service from Wexford and the sunny south-east as it passes the distant signal for Dalkey in 1954. This busy line has always had to accommodate both suburban trains stopping at all stations and long distance workings to Wexford and Rosslare. As will be noted from this photograph, CIE's AEC railcars unlike their GNR counterparts could form 8-car trains made up of four railcars and four intermediates.**
Both, Ian Allan Library

Above: **With Killiney Hill behind them, our intrepid Wexford GAA fans, seen on their way to the capital on page 51, head for home, their special hauled by a pair of the ubiquitous JI5s, the leading engine being No 188. Hopefully their team did well on the day.** Seán Kennedy

## BRAY

Centre: **Entering Bray in April 1948, yet another JI5 heads south but this time it is burning oil and not coal due to the severe coal shortages. A couple of GSR-built coaches make up the leading end of the train whilst an impressive gantry of semaphore signals is visible beyond.** SLS collection

Below: **At the south end of Bray station on 13th June 1954, I3 class 0-6-2 No 673 has just arrived from Greystones around the other side of the headland in the background. To the left of the train is what was at the time, Bray's locomotive shed. Today, although roofless, it is used as a stabling point for DART units.** Ian Allan Library

Top right: **Former GSWR 4-4-0 No 340 of GSR class D4 had just cleared the starting signal and was beginning its ascent of Bray Head en-route to Greystones, on this grey day in 1953. Note the gas tank wagon in the siding.** Ian Allan Library

Centre right: **Like Kildare, Bray station has a third road between the platforms. In this case, rather than being used for through running as is the case at Kildare, the centre road is most often used for stabling DART units as Bray is the terminus for the great majority of southbound DART services. On a Sunday afternoon in April 2002, recently reliveried DART unit No 8122 is at the head of a six-car set stabled on this road. The use of six-car formations, despite being technically feasible from the introduction of electric services, is a relatively recent phenomenon. The operators have been driven to this expedient by the popularity of the DART and the necessity to increase the size of some formations to reduce overcrowding.** Dónal Murray

Below: **At certain times of the year, Rosslare trains can be lightly loaded and may be formed of shorter sets as was the case with this up Rosslare to Connolly train seen at Bray in 1979, consisting of only three passenger coaches and two four-wheel heating/luggage vans headed by GM diesel, No 183. The 181 class loco hauling the train is certainly the diesel equivalent of the old J15s in terms of versatility. Most of these locomotives are still in service over three decades after their introduction in 1966.** Seán Kennedy

Above: **Having finally experienced what reliable diesels were like thanks to the arrival of 15 single-cab General Motors GL8's, the B121 class in 1961, CIE wisely ordered a double cab version, the JL8, from GM. These entered traffic in 1962/63. These 37 locomotives, together with their GM predecessors saved the railways from the operational disaster that the Crossley-engined Metro-Vick locomotives of the A and C classes had created. The B121s and B141s also had the distinct advantage of being equipped for operating in multiple, a** feature greatly used in their country of manufacture, the USA. Still brand new, **B145 in multiple with another B141 heads up what is evidently a publicity train due to its almost unbelievable cleanliness, at Bray in 1963.** Ian Allan Library

Below left: **When the DART opened to Bray in 1984, Greystones, which hitherto had a regular push-pull service, was left out in the cold somewhat. As a stop gap measure, a shuttle-service was set up to connect with a limited number of DART services. At first** the service was operated with a push-pull set, seen here in summer 1984 with locomotive No 232 at the rear. A J O'Rourke

Below right: **When the push-pull sets were withdrawn, there was no suitable stock to operate the shuttle, so a three-piece 80 class railcar set was hired from NIR. This remained in NIR livery although it did acquire Irish Rail logos for a while. It is seen here with the driving trailer leading, about to depart for Greystones in the summer 1988.** Dónal Murray

## GREYSTONES

Right: **To form a route from Bray to Greystones the Dublin & Wicklow Railway, under I K Brunel's guidance, had to cut, tunnel and bridge extensively around Bray Head. Coastal erosion over the years forced the route to be altered several times with new tunnels being bored. Today there are four tunnels on the formation between Bray and Greystones. Emerging from one of these in 1973 on a publicity run, is newly renumbered 001 class No 001 formerly A1r, with brand new British Rail Engineering designed Mk2 air conditioned coaches.** Ian Allan Library

Above: **Greystones station is very conveniently situated on the main street of the town it serves, unlike many Irish stations. In 1983, C201 class No 234 awaits the road with a suburban train for Bray and Howth.** A J O'Rourke

Right: **When the hired NIR set was sent home, no rolling stock was available to replace it and Greystones remained without any commuter service whatsoever until 2001 when the electric wires were eventually extended there and DART services could reach the town. On the first day of electric services, a pair of new Spanish-built 8200 class EMUs are at the platform.** Joe St Leger

## DRUMM BATTERY TRAINS

Left: **The DARTs were not the first electric trains to reach Bray. In the 1930s, UCD's Dr James Drumm, invented a powerful battery. Banks of these were used to power some railcars built at Inchicore works. In August 1933, Drumm battery railcars A and B, complete with an intermediate coach are on an official demonstration run, resplendent in the GSR's chocolate brown and cream livery. At the end of each journey the batteries required charging and this was carried out using the pantograph on the roof, seen under the footbridge.** Ian Allan Library

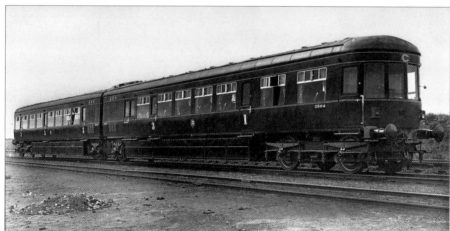

Centre: **In 1939 two more Drumm trains, C and D were built, the appearance of these units was more streamlined. In this works photograph, set C is in the GSR maroon colour scheme. The Drumm trains kept south-eastern suburban services going during the coal shortages of the Second World War. By 1949 however, the batteries were life expired and the units were converted to ordinary unpowered coaching stock.** Ian Allan Library

Below: **Bray's other route to the city, was closed amidst much controversy in December 1958. Commonly known as the Harcourt Street line after its Dublin terminus, its most important intermediate station was Dundrum where we see an ex-DSER 2-4-2 tank bound for Bray. In 2002 a double-track line is being built through this very station as part of Dublin's LUAS light rail system.** SLS collection

## HARCOURT STREET

Above: **Though it followed an inland route and served suburbs that were to mushroom in the 60s and 70s, the logic of the 1950s was that the Harcourt Street line duplicated the coastal route to Bray and thus had to close. Though the terminus occupied quite a large area, there was only one platform. This didn't really cause that much of a problem as services were not as frequent as on the more heavily used coastal route to Westland Row.**
SLS collection

Centre: **In this early 1950s view of Harcourt Street station, to the right of the steam locomotives, is a former Drumm battery train, either A or B, its batteries now removed, in use as a loco hauled trailer set.**
Midland Publishing collection

Bottom: **Harcourt Street station was in its dying days in December 1958 when this photograph of an Inchicore-built AEC railcar was taken. Six of these railcars, powered by two 125hp AEC engines were built at Inchicore, in 1956, when O V S Bulleid, was in charge. Within a few years all had been converted to powered intermediates and some ended their days as un-powered intermediates in five-piece push-pull sets, in the 1970s.**
Ian Allan Library

# INCHICORE WORKS

Above: **Probably one of the largest single-user industrial complexes in the country, Inchicore works, which opened in 1846, is located 1¾ miles out from Kingsbridge/Heuston on the GSWR main line. Covering approximately 73 acres, 'the works', as it is commonly known amongst railway staff, has manufactured just about everything in its lifetime from brake blocks to locomotives and even components for armoured cars and munitions during war times. From GSR days until the early 1970s, buses were also manufactured at Inchicore. At its peak over 2000 people** were employed there, although nowadays this number is substantially less and many of the workshops are now idle. It is over forty years since Inchicore works turned out its last locomotive and its primary function is now that of a maintenance depot. Prominent in this late 1970s aerial view of Inchicore, is Diesel Shop No 1 in the left centre of the photograph. Formerly known as the erecting shop, this is the place where the most powerful steam locomotives ever to run in Ireland, the three B1a class 4-6-0s, were built in 1939/40. The last class of new-built, as opposed to re-built, diesels emerged from here in 1962/63, in the form of the E421 class of diesel hydraulics. Still an impressive place, Inchicore has adopted to the changing needs of the railway system over the years, from steam to diesel and, since the initiation of the DART services, the staff at Inchicore have also had to learn the skills necessary to maintain and repair electric units. CIE/Iarnród Éireann

Right: **The views on this page, were taken outside the works and cover a period of over 50 years. The Eucharistic Congress came to Ireland in 1932. This was an event of huge importance for the devoutly Catholic majority of the population. In that year, the Cardinal Legate paid a visit to Killarney. The GSR laid on a special train for his trip hauled by 4-4-0 No 328, seen here at Inchicore, adorned with papal flags and insignia. The train included the former Royal saloons of the GSWR and the MGWR, together with a dining saloon and a brake coach. The GSR's Traffic Manager accompanied the train and the driver and fireman wore rosettes and cap bands in the papal colours.** GSR/Iarnród Éireann

Centre: In **this early 1950s view, B2a class 4-6-0 No 406, is powering a set of GNR teak liveried coaches, at the time when the 'Enterprise' service was extended to Cork. This locomotive had taken over from a GNR engine at Amiens Street. To the right of the train is Inchicore's ornate castellated running shed, which is also visible in the previous photograph. To the left of the train is Inchicore's signal cabin, itself an ornate structure in the style of the architecture on the other side of the tracks. This cabin remained in service until 2002.** Des McGlynn collection

Bottom: **In 1984, a DART unit paid its first visit to Inchicore works, not under its own power of course but towed behind a small GM driven by Bernard C Byrne. Whilst Fairview depot carries out all of the day to day maintenance on the DART units, they need to visit Inchicore for major work, such as general overhauls and refurbishment, wheel turning or painting. Passing the 141 class locomotive and the DART unit is a Shelton Abbey (Arklow) to Marino Point (Cork) empty ammonia train hauled by, No 029.** Bernard C Byrne

Top left: **On these pages we will look at some of the steam locomotive classes which were either built or maintained at Inchicore over the decades. The first, and the oldest, is not actually an Inchicore product. No 36 was built for the GSWR by Bury, Curtis & Kennedy in 1847 and incredibly is still in existence today, preserved under cover inside the entrance to Cork Kent station. This remarkable survivor from the commencement of services on the GSWR main line in the 1840s, is seen here outside the old running shed in Inchicore in 1958, on display for the delegates to an international transport congress held there in that year.** CIE/Iarnród Éireann

Centre left: **Also on display on the same occasion was 0-6-0 No 184, of the GSWR 101 class, the J15s of the GSR. This locomotive was built in Inchicore in 1880. As befits Ireland's most numerous class of steam engines, two of these machines have been preserved. The other preserved J15, No 186, was actually built a year earlier than No 184. However, No 186 was rebuilt with a superheated Belpaire boiler and has a larger tender with inside springs. No 184 is closer to her original condition than her sister, No 186. Both locomotives are in the care of the Railway Preservation Society of Ireland.** CIE/Iarnród Éireann

Below: **One of the more unusual products of the works was a small class of carriage engines originally used on the Castleisland branch in County Kerry. No 92 was built in 1881. When traffic on the branch became too great for these machines, two of the three were rebuilt as tank locos. No 92 however, remained in original condition and was used for many years to ferry officials and visitors between Kingsbridge and Inchicore.** Ian Allan Library

Above: **It must have taken quite a bit of effort to turn a 500 class on Inchicore's turntable as is evidenced by the stance of the crew member hard at work. Resplendent in the attractive green livery that was applied in early CIE days in the late 1940s and early 1950s to certain locomotives, No 502 has just come off duty from a Cork express judging by it's empty tender.** Seán Kennedy

Centre right: **One of the few locomotives constructed during the GSR period, 0-6-2 tank No 674 of class I3, looks absolutely splendid in CIE green livery, as it prepares to return to duty on the DSER section, after overhaul at Inchicore.** Ian Allan Library

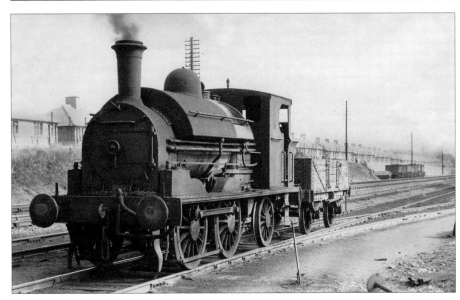

Bottom right: **Built in 1914 to the design of R E L Maunsell, a Dublin man whose locos for the Southern Railway in Britain in the 1920s and 30s are better known than his work at Inchicore, *Sambo*, was the pilot locomotive at Inchicore works virtually up to the end of steam in the early 1960s. *Sambo* was known by name only, it was never allocated a number by any of its three owners, the GSWR, the GSR or CIE.** Ian Allan Library

Above: **For the 1958 congress, Inchicore put on quite a display of motive power. In this photograph all of the principal new diesel classes from A to C are lined up along with one other unique locomotive, O V S Bulleid's No CC1, commonly known as the 'Turf Burner'. A development of the experimental 'Leader' class machines which had already manifestly failed in** Britain, having cost British Railways dearly, this Irish version of the concept, designed to burn the country's only indigenous fuel, had no more success. No. CC1 is actually in steam in this view, next to it is a Metro-Vick A class, a BRCW/Sulzer B101 class, the Inchicore-built B113 and finally a Metro-Vick C class in its original silver livery. CIE/Iarnród Éireann

Below: **Posing in front of Sancton Wood's running shed at Inchicore, is Metro-Vick diesel, A7. It is thought the tower was used for observing trains in the early days of signalling. The Crossley diesel engines in these locos were totally unreliable. Only when Inchicore rebuilt all 60 with GM power units, did they achieve their true potential. Ian Allan Library**

Top right: **In this 1931 view of the carriage shop at Inchicore, a marvellous variety of rolling stock can be seen. The timber frames for Drumm battery train A are under construction in the centre of the picture. To the left of this is a ex-GSWR compartment coach. Ahead of of this standard gauge vehicle are two narrow gauge carriages. The first is a six wheel West Clare section carriage, beyond this is one of the distinctive bogie coaches with end verandas which were used on the Cavan & Leitrim narrow gauge line.** GSR/Iarnród Éireann

Centre right: **The original carriage shop was destroyed by a fire towards the end of the twentieth century and was rebuilt with such architectural style that it has been unofficially christened 'the Gare de Nord', due to a vague resemblance to the famous Paris station's overall roof no doubt. In 1998 the carriage shop's primary activity was maintenance and refurbishment and here we see a Cravens coach of 1963 vintage being beautifully turned out in its 35th year of service.** Dónal Murray

Below: **Resting on a siding adjacent to Diesel No 1 in September 2000 and awaiting trials, is a brand new 8500 class DART, not long in from Japan. These units are intended for outer suburban services now that the DART has been extended to Malahide and Greystones and are the first DART units to feature intermediate coaches.** Dónal Murray

Above: **Diesel No 1 in Inchicore has been the site for the manufacture, assembly and maintenance of most of the varied locomotives and railcars which have run on the CIE system, both standard and narrow gauge, since the early 1950s. Constructed in 1935 as part of the GSR's extension programme, it had up to ten overhead cranes with capacities varying from seven to 40 tons. From the beginning of the diesel era, until relatively recently, all heavy repair work and rebuilding was carried out here. Today the shop is much quieter as a lot of its former activities have been transferred to the nearby Diesel No 2. Some work has also been outsourced. In the foreground can be seen the bogie repair section and on the wall in the background just beyond the cranes is a 1960s mural depicting a cutaway view of an A class locomotive.** Dónal Murray

Centre left: **Many of Inchicore's trades people benefited from the in-house training in the Inchicore Apprentice School. At one time several generations of families could be found employed in the works. In this view taken in the 1980s of the now closed school, budding sheet-metal workers are busy learning their trade.** CIE/Iarnród Éireann

Bottom left: **The trades and skills needed at Inchicore were incredibly varied. Like all the great railway works, Inchicore was virtually self-sufficient. Here we see fitters and electricians at work on a Mk 3 coach in the carriage shop.** Iarnród Éireann

Above: **Being a self-sufficient place and occupying a site the size of a small town, Inchicore has its own fire-service, ambulance and security police.** Iarnród Éireann

Above right and right: **In 1984, GM No 145 was hijacked by terrorists on a freight working in Northern Ireland. The driver was taken out of the locomotive and a bomb placed in the cab. The results were catastrophic and it was initially thought that No 145 was a complete write-off. However, one very experienced metal-fabricator thought otherwise. Over three years later the crew that brought No 184 back to life, were photographed in front of the completely rebuilt locomotive. The man who said it could be done, Denis Murray the author's father, is standing in the centre of the group in the foreground, directly under the loco's number.** CIE/Iarnród Éireann

Below: **Another view inside Diesel No 1, this time in September 2000, with 201 and 071 class locomotives in for repairs.** Dónal Murray

# PORTS AND PINTS

Above: **The GSWR route to the North Wall and Amiens Street was used from 1937 until 1973 by all former MGWR section trains. In the late 1960s CIE was still operating its famous 'Radio Train' in the summer to certain destinations such as Galway. Featuring a radio studio coach broadcasting to its passengers, the 'Radio Train' was popular for many years. Heading west at Claude Road on a fine** summer's morning, B172, complete with headboard, hauls the train which includes an ex-GSR restaurant car built in 1935.

Below left: **Looking almost identical to the B141 class, the B181 class, introduced in 1966, were more powerful by 150hp. When brand new B187, is seen here hauling its long goods train out of North Wall bound for Dundalk.**

Below right: **The alternative route to the North Wall from points south-west and west was via the MGWR canal-side route. This also gave access to Amiens Street via a lifting bridge over the canal at Newcomen Junction and a short steep incline up to the station. Photographs of the original bridge being raised are rare. Luckily Bernard C Byrne was on hand to record this event during the late 1960s.** All, Bernard C Byrne

Top left: **The MGWR had its own yard at the North Wall. Seen on St Patrick's Day 1950 this was still a busy place as Woolwich Mogul No 395 prepares to depart on a goods for the west.** Ian Allan Library

Top right: **In 1971 the Woolwich locomotives were long gone and former C class No B204 was busy shunting in Midland Yard.** Des McGlynn

Above left: **Nine years earlier in February 1962, E411 a Maybach-engined Inchicore built locomotive which entered service on 25th January 1958, is seen climbing up the bank from the Midland yard to East Wall Junction, where connection was made between the North Wall lines and the former GNR main line.** Alan Roome

Above: **On another cold February day in 1962, an Inchicore built locomotive from an earlier era, Coey designed J9 class 0-6-0 No 354, dating from 1903, is recorded shunting in front of the Smith & Pearson's works at the North Wall.** Alan Roome

Above: **Part of the extensive network of sidings at North Wall between Church Road Junction and the Point Depot is shown in this photograph. The Liebherr factory in Killarney had fabricated a massive crane for a North American customer. It was taken by rail to Dublin port for export.**
Bernard C Byrne

Below left: **In later years, a large warehouse was built to cater for sundries traffic at the Midland yard. Sundries traffic had been gradually declining when it was decided to rebrand it as 'Raillink' in the early 1990s. It would soldier on for another few years before the traffic and the building ceased to exist.** Iarnród Éireann

Below right: **Another feature of this area, and the Dublin skyline, which has disappeared, is this gasometer. It was still there in the summer of 1988, when this view of the former London North Western yard at North Wall was taken. Part of this site is to be incorporated in the Spencer Dock redevelopment.** Dónal Murray

Above: **With the redevelopment of the dockland area clearly visible in the background, the massive crane for handling containers at the former LNWR yard was photographed on the 18th February 2002.** Dónal Murray

Above right: **Moving eastwards, a double track tramway extends down Alexandra Road. Zinc ore from Tara Mines has been exported from here since 1977. On a winter afternoon in 1995, an 071 class locomotive leaves Dock Board property at Alexandra Road bound for Tara Mines with a rake of empties.** Des McGlynn

Right: **Coastal Containers were until relatively recently another customer served by the Alexandra Road tramway.** Iarnród Éireann

Below: **The bulk of new rolling stock for Iarnród Éireann is landed at the North Wall, close to the formerly railway-owned Point Depot. In August 2000, a new Japanese-built 8500 class DART has just been landed and is being towed by a 141 class loco to Inchicore.** Iarnród Éireann

Photographs on the opposite page:

Top: **The first DART units, the 8100 class, arrived at the same location some 17 years earlier in 1983. Those units came from Germany, where they were manufactured by Linke Hoffman Busch at Salzgitter.** Ian Allan Picture Library

Bottom: **The second part of this chapter illustrates one of the most fascinating industrial railway systems ever to operate in Ireland. It also dealt with perhaps the country's most famous product. Back in 1957 the GNRB and CIE were not the only ones to have a railway system in Dublin. The city's Guinness brewery, boasted a substantial dual-gauge railway system. Photographed from the top of Kingsbridge station a portion of the 5ft 3in gauge system is seen with the line which connected the brewery's railway to the national rail network at Kingsbridge, passing through the gate in the foreground. Both GNR and CIE wagons can be seen in**

the sidings in the left foreground. One of the Guinness owned Hudswell Clarke diesel shunters is in the centre of the picture. To its left is one of the special broad gauge wagons designed and built in Dublin to allow the brewery's 1ft 10in narrow gauge steam locomotives to haul broad gauge wagons on 5ft 3in gauge tracks. Guinness Ireland Archives

Above: **As well as having a connection to Kingsbridge which allowed standard gauge wagons to be brought up to the sidings seen opposite, there was an extensive network of 1ft 10in narrow gauge tracks in and around the brewery. The steam locomotives which worked on these tracks were designed and built in Dublin. They were constructed at the Cork Street Foundry between 1887 and 1921 to the design of Samuel Geoghegan, a Guinness engineer. These were ingenious machines. Their cylinders were mounted above the boiler and the wheels were driven via an intermediate crankshaft. They were**

designed to be craned into specially built wagons of 5ft 3in gauge. Through complex gearing they could drive the wheels of these wagons, and were thus able to work trains on both gauges. In this wonderfully evocative view, one of the Geoghegan narrow gauge locomotives has brought a train of barrels of stout to the wharf on the river at Victoria Quay, beside the brewery. The barrels are being transferred to a barge which will take them down to the North Wall for onward shipment, probably to slake the thirsts of Guinness drinkers on the other side of the Irish Sea. Although specially built to navigate under the low Liffey bridges, at times the barges could get stuck at high tide between bridges, delaying their journeys. To those who have only known the city in the decades since the motor car has become king, the lack of traffic on the quays in this view, is astonishing. Both, Guinness Ireland Archives

Above: **Before the Hudswell Clarke diesels seen earlier, arrived on the scene, a pair of 0-4-0 saddletank steam locomotives from the same maker worked the 5ft 3in lines in the brewery and made the transfer trips to Kingsbridge yard. One of these engines is seen here beside one of the Geoghegan locomotives in a 5ft 3in gauge haulage truck. In the foreground a section of 1ft 10in gauge track crosses the 5ft 3in line in front of the Geoghegan locomotive.**

Left: **In 1954 the Geoghegan locomotives were still hard at work. Barrels of Guinness were transferred onto the barges moored at Victoria Quay, by the crane seen here beside Geoghegan locomotive No 24. Note the shine off the mens' shoes. Guinness insisted that their staff were of neat appearance at all times.** Both, Guinness Ireland Archives

Top: **In 1957, the Geoghegan designed steam locomotives were superseded by a fleet of Planet diesels. Locomotive No 34 is seen here with its train of flat wagons laden with barrels on Victoria Quay, whilst still quite new.**

Above: **In 1958, the last narrow gauge train operated out of the cooperage yard. As a Planet diesel hauls its laden train across the yard, someone has thoughtfully painted 'RIP' on the tiny tank wagon in front of the locomotive. The rest of the narrow gauge system remained in use until**

**1975. Though there is no longer a tramway between the brewery and the yard at Kingsbridge, that closed in 1965, Guinness is still distributed across Ireland by rail.**
Both, Guinness Ireland Archives

Above left: **An essential ingredient of this most famous of Irish beverages is malt. In this photograph taken in 1950, malt is seen being emptied from narrow gauge hoppers into the grain elevator.**

Above right: **The narrow gauge system was on two levels. Originally these were connected by a hydraulic lift but this was later replaced by a spiral tunnel. Narrow gauge tracks actually ran down some of the side streets around the St James Gate Brewery. In a view dating from around 1957, a Planet diesel is seen pulling grain wagons down Robert Street on the upper level of the system.**

Below: **A Hudswell Clarke 0-4-0s leaves the brewery heading for Kingsbridge with a laden train. When this connection was closed, one of the two steam locomotives was presented by Guinness to the Railway Preservation Society of Ireland. It has since been used to give steam train rides at the RPSI's base at Whitehead in County Antrim and has seen service at the Downpatrick Railway Museum.**

Photograph on page 77: **In another marvellously evocative scene from the past, a transfer working from the brewery, with flagmen front and rear, hauled by one of the Hudswell Clarke diesels, rumbles down St John's Road. Given the changes to this part of the city since the 1960s, the road is now a busy dual carriageway, it is hard to believe that this was once an everyday scene. Traffic is building up behind the train as it enters Kingsbridge yard and two young boys, probably grandfathers by now, look on at the spectacle with fascination.** All four pictures on these pages, Guinness Ireland Archives

# THE FUTURE

Left: **Our glimpse of the future, begins with a look to the past. Dublin once had the biggest tramway system in these islands. Latterly run by CIE, the trams were abandoned in favour of buses, seen as the answer to the capital's future needs. The final tram routes, serving Dalkey and Terenure, were closed in 1949. This view shows trams inside Blackrock depot, the building still extant today, is seen shortly before the final closure in 1949.**
F N T Lloyd Jones

Below: **Trams from Terenure on route number 15, terminated at Nelson's Pillar in the centre of O'Connell Street. Not far from the end of their journeys, two 15s are seen here, a Standard type and a Luxury car, both constructed at the Dublin United Tramway Company's works at Spa Road in Inchicore.** Dublin Transportation Office

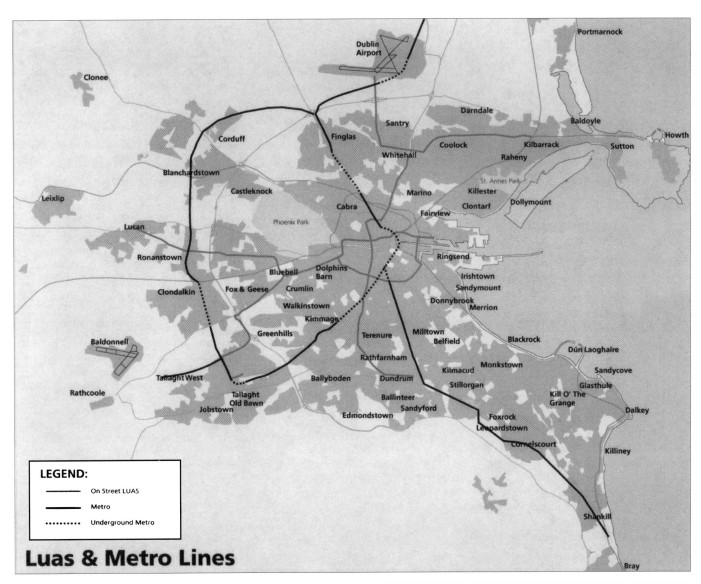

## Luas & Metro Lines

**LEGEND:**

―――――― On Street LUAS

━━━━━ Metro

·············· Underground Metro

Above: **Things have now come full circle since Dublin's last trams ran in the 1940s. The capital is now so gridlocked with the very motor traffic seen as the way forward then, that rail-based transport and modern trams are now viewed by the powers that be, as a very important part of the solution to the capital's transportation problems. A whole network of LUAS light rail and Metro lines is being planned as part of of a belated attempt to keep the city on the move.** Railway Procurement Agency

Right: **Kingsbridge station, where we began our photographic journey at the start of this book, will have once again be served by trams when LUAS line A from Tallaght to Middle Abbey Street opens.**
Railway Procurement Agency

Above left: **LUAS light rail vehicles still had bubble wrap on some of their internal fittings when the author paid a visit to the nearly complete Red Cow maintenance facility for LUAS line A on the 19th January 2002. These vehicles employ state of the art technology and will bring modern transportation to Dublin, the likes of which have not been seen before. The depot itself is quite self-contained and includes servicing ramps, stores, a wheel lathe, overhead cranes and a bogie wash.**

Above right: **On the 4th February 2002, a considerable section of track was nearly complete on the Ballymount Road between the Red Cow depot and Tallaght. The entire system is being built to the European standard gauge of 4ft 8½, with the future disposal value of stock and the ability to purchase off the shelf vehicles in mind. This initial section of track was being used to test the newly arrived light rail vehicles.** Both, Dónal Murray

Below: **When the bridge in this montage, over the Grand Canal on the old Harcourt Street line alignment, is built, rail transportation in the capital will really have come full circle. Since the last CIE passenger train passed over the canal in December 1958, the wisdom of this closure has been frequently debated. By 2004 the Harcourt Street line, or at least a great part of it, will finally be reopened for business, a sure sign of the bright future for rails around Dublin.** Railway Procurement Agency